*"Except the Lord

Build the House"*

PS 127:1a

Copyright 2019

All Scripture quotations, unless otherwise noted are taken from the King James Version of the Holy Bible.

All rights reserved. No part of this book may be reproduced or transmitted in any form or by any means, electronic or mechanical, including photocopying, or recording, or by any information storage and retrieval system without written permission from publisher or author. The only exception is brief quotations for review.

For information address:
J2B Publishing LLC
4251 Columbia Park Road
Pomfret, MD 20675
www.J2BLLC.com

Printed and bound in the United States of America.

This book is set in Garamond.

ISBN: 978-1-948747-45-5

"Except the Lord Build the House"
PS 127:1a

Randy and Cheryl Heddings

J2B PUBLISHING

DEDICATION

God is the source of what we do. It seems almost vain to dedicate a book to Him but it is through His hand we were and are allowed to do the things He has chosen us to do. God is indeed the Alpha and the Omega. God is indeed the great provider for us all. Through this book we hope to be involved in many more church plants.

Cheryl, my beloved wife, and our youngest daughter, Jessica, stood in support of the work the Lord called us into. It was their support and encouragement during times that appeared to everyone else to be gloomy and dim that enabled us to persevere until we saw the results the Lord had promised. Their stand on the solid rock of faith, Jesus the Christ, helped me to laugh during tough times and resulted in our writing about church planting from a personal perspective.

My family at home for their prayers and willingness to help us see the fulfillment of God's work through us. My parents, Ray and Barbara Heddings, my brother and sister-in-law and my sister and brother-in-law made it much more enjoyable for to serve the Lord.

All the people God sent into our lives during this time period. Their help was crucial to the work we accomplished. We were encouraged as the Holy Spirit revealed things to them that stretched their faith and belief structure and by their willingness to serve God completely.

Table of Contents

DEDICATION v
INTRODUCTION ix
CHAPTER ONE 1
CHAPTER TWO 9
CHAPTER THREE 21
CHAPTER FOUR 29
CHAPTER FIVE 37
CHAPTER SIX 45
CHAPTER SEVEN 51
CHAPTER EIGHT 61
CHAPTER NINE 67
Meet the Authors 72

INTRODUCTION

Psalm 127:1a, *"Except the Lord build the house, they labour in vain that build it…"* (KJV)

As Cheryl and I had the Lord move upon us about going into the ministry, back in 1998, we saw our entire world changing directions. We were a family that went to church and tried the best we could to serve God. We had a successful business that allowed us to raise our children. Cheryl was Catholic and I was brought up in yet another denomination. Both families attended church regularly and we were brought up seeing service to the Lord going on through the families, for the most part.

Having surrendered to God and accepting Jesus, as the Lord and Savior of my life in June 1974, at a revival in a small Baptist Church in Prichard, Al, my relationship with God, through Christ began to grow. It was something to this day I cannot explain in its entirety and probably never will be able to do.

Cheryl grew up in a Catholic home and when we were married, we agreed to raise our children in the Catholic tradition.

Cheryl's career led her into sales and marketing and mine was in the military. We both can look back into our lives and see the preparation God was doing even then. Our oldest daughter was in her senior year of High School and the Lord spoke to me and said now is the time. The intensity of which I heard this call was something that I will never forget and knew I must answer!

I told Cheryl about my calling the next morning on the way to work. I figured, where could she go at 70 MPH? She was a captive to what had to be said. Her immediate reaction was to call the Priest, who couldn't really relate to the situation either. She knew and I knew, our lives were forever changed, as we had grown to know them. The next issue was where would we get started? We made a few calls and began the process. Speaking from experience, Catholics and Protestants do things very much different in a call into the ministry.

What about the obstacles in the way? What about the house, the business and the other investments we had? As I prayed about them, the Lord brought to mind the scriptures about the rich young ruler. He told him to sell everything, give it to the poor and follow Me! (Mark 10:17-31) What do you do? Can you just imagine everything you have strived to do gone! At a time of apparent comfort in life and BOOM! It's got to go! Was it a struggle for us? Of course, it was! Again, the Lord led me to the scriptures about the calling of the disciples. He said, "straightway" or immediately, they followed after Him. (Matthew 4:18-22) Remember the big catch in Luke 5: 1-11? Jesus called the disciples after perhaps one of the biggest catches they had ever made. They had held back on some of that catch too in their reluctance to do as Christ had instructed. They were instructed to lower their nets but after the discussion it was said, *"nevertheless, we will lower the net."* I am convinced Jesus knows our every capability and it is our hesitation that stops us from receiving His all for us. Nevertheless, they left the family business at a certain time of prosperity, denying the riches of the world to follow Him. The Lord asks, what would it prosper a man to have everything and then loose his own soul? (Matthew 16:26)

This was a new dimension for us. The house went, the extra cars went the business went and the geographical changes began to take place. The time of sacrifice had become intensified. Do you really think we can predict what sacrifices God will put on us? I am in solid belief that nothing can exist that we are not willing to sacrifice in service of Him.

We find in the Book of Acts that many sold their houses for the work of the ministry. (Acts 2:42-47) What a call to commitment. We find in Acts chapter 5: 1-11) about a couple that tried to be deceptive about their commitment to the work of the Lord for perhaps personal gain.

"I am crucified with Christ: nevertheless I live; yet not I, but Christ liveth in me: and the life I now live in the flesh I live by the faith of the Son of God, who loved me, and gave himself for me." (Galatians 2:20, KJV)

This is the new dimension that we had to arrive within to begin to do God's work and be able to see fruit being brought forth. It was not a mere matter of just saying ok God; you can do what you want with me, providing I am in full agreement. This was a matter of doing what God wanted done regardless of the pain and sacrifice it might cause us. After all, I am not required to jump up and hang on a cross for my sin, although I must be willing. My sacrifice is done through submission to God and doing it God's way. It took that same commitment that Moses and Isaiah had as they spoke with God and then answered, "Here am I Lord, send me." (Isaiah 6:8) No one needs to tell us about the times and struggles that God is putting you through relating to a call into the ministry. We have been there. It was in a fruitful time of this worldly life that we were called into the area of the unknown. The Lord says in His Word; walk by faith and not by sight. Easy to say but hard to do! Surrender to God and denying ourselves was what it takes to serve Him and to continue to serve Him.

We are not where we are today in a walk with Him because of who we are, it is all because of Who He IS! Being called to begin new works for God was a growth process for us. We started our journey into ministry, after serving as an associate Pastor in central

Texas and then moved into a Pastoral role in the Ozark Mountains of southwest Missouri. Many changes took place and the Holy Spirit training became intense. I believed when we left off into the Pastoral ministry that we were up and ready to the challenge. I never could have been more right and wrong at the same time. We were ready to go to the Pastoral role in ministry but were extremely wrong about being ready for what the spiritual battlefield was to bring to us.

The long and short of the lesson learned was, seeing the things the Lord was seeing from His throne above and what was happening within the churches. God loves His people and His church. Since I am convinced, there are things that God is not particularly pleased with in the church, as a young Pastor, I thought that change could be brought about through speaking God's word and it would bring forth the necessary correction. The understanding that the Pastor is the spiritual leader of the church was dispelled quickly and very abruptly. In a long prayer session with the Lord one night, while in deep agony, He spoke to me very vividly as I asked Him, why? What had I done to fail Him and the church? He took me straight to His Word where He says that *"behold, I refine you not as silver but in the furnace of affliction."* (Isaiah 48:10) He goes on to say that He will do it for His glory for His glory will not be shared with another. He had to do something that only He could do within our lives and within His church. Things happening that we could not see any sense. It was a strong spiritual battle that was raging.

My first belief of being a Pastor was that the Pastor received the vision, they cast the vision to the church, and then, the Pastor, being the leader led the charge! This is the Bull in a China cabinet expression of leadership. People do not tend to be led that way. Remember, Jesus had reason to call us children. Even God refers to us as rebellious. (Ezekiel 12:2-3) That belief had to change in me! It was during the time of church planting the Lord revealed to me that Pastoral ministry was something that I really knew nothing about but was used as a learning tool for us. We had to see the things the Lord wanted to see done and we had to learn how to do it. The philosophy about leading the charge changed dramatically. Now, I believe, a Pastor does in fact get a vision, the church also has a vision, the Pastor shares that vision and then, the pastor must retreat to the prayer closet and seek God on how He would have it accomplished and watch God build the House through His people.

As we arrived in central Texas to plant the works the Lord had spoken to us about, we were still riding on the wave He placed us on leaving the Pastorate. God had, in only the way He can, provided for us to move and be able to safeguard the few things we still have. That was the end of that part of it though. There was supposed to be a house for us and it didn't even exist, adding meaning to what the Lord says about trusting no man. Even as we went off into church planting, I was still trying to ensure the safety and security of my family. After all, the Lord says it is our duty to do so. (1 Timothy 5:8)

All of my plans failed and we had to lean on God. To be perfectly honest, we tried to figure out how to get out of there as quick as we could but there was no escape. I even tried to find a Pastoral position in the local area and work there. No way! I did have the privilege of filling in for a couple of Sundays at a couple of churches and made some great friends that later played important roles in church planting with us. But there was no escape! The Lord had brought us to the point that we must make that ultimate decision to sell out or suffer the consequences. As I sat in a church pew on our third Sunday in Texas, the Lord spoke to me and asked me how I liked sitting in that pew! He went on to tell me that if I continued to disobey Him that is where I would sit until I decided to follow Him. I would be left standing on the shoreline so to speak. That brought the immediate response that should He want the work, He and He alone would have to provide. We had no money, no denominational support and no friends in the town to speak of. The ones we had didn't do the things they had promised. God would simply have to provide.

During a time of prayer, the Lord and I were discussing the why's of me in church planting or apostolic ministry. Understanding the ministry of God, through Christ, and believing that God doesn't ever change and that Apostles and Prophets still exist today, this discussion was one that I will never forget. The Lord revealed to me that only those that have been through His refining fires would ever be called to get into apostolic ministry and church planting. His words of encouragement were simply that it is the only place that one can and does serve in the fullness of the five-fold ministry at one time. Not only was it encouragement, it became a heavy burden in doing His work. This work would never have been possible without God in the lead and my family's support.

In speaking with the Lord about the lack of support and money, the Lord reminded me of what He said about He owns the world and the fullness thereof. (Psalms 50:12) He is the only provider! (Philippians 4:19) We looked at a local sales paper and right on the front page, there were some church pews for sale. We called and inquired about them. The minister asked what they were going to be for and we simply told him a new work. He and his church donated the pews. Their church also donated a piano and piano bench along with a podium. Another local family donated us some land for the work but still no place to meet. One of the people from a church, where we filled in, was speaking with us and we told him about the vision the Lord gave us. As the Lord would have it, they happed to own a strip mall in the very town we were in and offered it free for the establishment of a work for God. God placed everything in order in less than 30 days to begin a work in central Texas.

As we were cleaning the building for the church, Cheryl was inside and I was cleaning letters off the glass in front, I was again crying to God about the situation. We were living in an 8X17 ft camping trailer, with no running water and no air conditioning. (we lived in it for 7 months) We had to go to a shop that we were helping a man get back into shape to sell so we could take a shower. For those that have never been to central Texas, using a fan would be the logical solution but, in a small trailer in 100 degree plus weather, it is a lot like being in a convection oven. I was telling God all about our situation, as if He didn't already know, when He began to remind me of when His people were coming back from captivity. He reminded me that before they were allowed to build the house of the Lord, they had to first build an altar and sacrifice to the Lord. (Ezekiel 3:2) As I spoke with Him, He told me to take care of His business for Him and He would take care of mine. I believe this is a statement that we all need to be reminded of as we trudge through this old world, knowing that God will provide as we stay with Him.

For nearly two years, God provided for this family and what needed to be done in His works at the same time. I keep referring to works as there were a total of 4 works established and a distribution warehouse that supplied food, clothing and used furniture to those in need. He also allowed us time to do mission work in East Central Mexico. (Acts 1:8)

My friends, I knew nothing about planting a church and still know very little. What we have to share with you are the things the Lord has shown to us. Perhaps this book may make you a little uncomfortable from time to time. I am not trying to bring forth anything other than what God has revealed. I will be using terms like, God showed me, as in visions and dreams. He spoke to me, as in audible voices. He woke me through sounds, and other things that may seem foreign to many as we reveal our encounters in growth through a relationship with God through Christ Jesus. I pray this book may serve as an encouragement to those that have been called and sent forth to do the Lord's work. I pray that it will reveal that God will do all He has promised to do for us. Remember, God is no respecter of persons and what He has done in central Texas, He will continue to do all over the world for those that will lay down their worldly possessions and follow Him! (Romans 2:11)

CHAPTER ONE

For God so loved the world - John 3:16

John 3:16; *"For God so loved the world, that He gave His only begotten Son, that whosoever believeth in Him should not perish, but have everlasting life."*

For God so loved the world that He gave! (John 3:16) What a profound statement we find in John! God has given and given to His creation. God established covenant after covenant with man, not because God has failed but because we have failed to submit and follow Him. God gave up what we would consider to be His most prize possession. He gave up what HE says to be the Very best and His very best did it willingly for us. Yes, He did it for me and He did it for you. We sometimes get caught up in the belief that if God had to do it all over again, He would do it again just for me. No, God says that Christ died once for every man. (Hebrews 9:26) There will not be another chance except Him. The deal and last covenant has been made by God to man and it is up to us to accept or reject His sacrifice for us. God longs for a restored relationship with His people. He has opened salvation to any that will come. (John 1:12) He has issued the call to every man or else He wouldn't have died for us all. No man is excluded from entering into God's kingdom and fellowship except man makes the decision. In the scriptures it is written that in the fullness of time, He came. In the fullness of time, in a man's heart, the Christ will come!

I say these things to remind us that before we can actually get our there and do God's work, we have got to have this issue of personal salvation settled and rooted deeply. (Colossians 2:6-8) There will be many that will scrutinize what you are doing. Other ministers will discourage you! It will be a time that the only pillar you can lean on is the Rock of your Salvation, Christ Jesus. As we arrived in Texas and were seeking association with a group of churches, the first question I was asked was, without any money, how long do you expect to be here? (Matthew 6:24) There even will have been others that have tried to do a work before you and perhaps were not successful in their endeavors for one reason or another. We must be absolutely sure that we are grounded in our faith and that we are secure in the arms of our loving God! We must be equally sure God has spoken to us about planting the new work!

It will take all you have and the very best of it! It will take more than we had, we would find out later. The Lord tells us that His grace is sufficient for in our weakness He is made strong. We will do well as long as we stay in that broken spirit willing to be molded into what the Lord would have us to be. A man that had been called into the ministry, called me one morning and asked, where in the gospels "for God so loved the world" was located? I told him it was in John 3:16. He was relieved to find out it wasn't in Matthew's Gospel because he had spent the entire night reading it and searching. His first message was on John 3:16! He said that God did not give His cow, best sheep or goat nor His best cowboy boots but His Only Begotten Son! All the worldly things matter not to God, just our soul. He doesn't want us in part. He wants all of us and wants us to give of ourselves willingly.

Bringing in new paradigms into an established area is going to bring fire from the religious people that have not allowed changes in their own churches. The new work will affect theirs as God's work is glorified.

This brings us up to the area of commitment. How committed do we want to be verses how committed does God want us to be? God has much to say about our commitment. He tells us in the writings of Hebrews, *"Ye have not yet resisted unto blood, striving against sin."* (Hebrews 12:4) Jesus gave up His blood to redeem us and He gave it all! Here we hear the words of the Lord reminding us that we still have a ways to go in getting through this lifetime and drawing closer to

Him. God has called us to lay these things of the world aside, even if it hurts in service to Him!

We are today, riding on a wave of grace that simply does not exist within the church. (Jude 4) We have a tendency to believe that God understands and His grace will cover our disobedience and lack of commitment. Although there is nothing but the grace of God that is going to get us into heaven and in the presence of our Savior Christ Jesus, God also admonishes us that faith without works is dead. (James 2:17) We must have change in our lives and churches for God to lead the work. There is no gray area as has been taught in times past. There are no really simple messages that will make our life easy. The relationship we have with Christ will cause us to have a changed life, forever.

"For there are certain men crept in unawares, who were before of old ordained to this condemnation, ungodly men, turning the grace of our God into lasciviousness, and denying the only Lord God, and our Lord Jesus Christ." Jude verse 4 (KJV)

"Thy prophets have seen vain and foolish things for thee: and they have not discovered thine iniquity, to turn away the captivity; but have seen for thee false burdens and causes of banishment." Lamentations 2:14 (KJV)

Many ministers today are plagued with a spirit of fear against telling people what is going on between them and God, as the Lord is revealing it. People are struggling to be made free from the bondage and baggage that they accumulate along life's journey. Do them a favor and be obedient to what God would have you to do. Many times, people are fully aware of what they hear but need confirmation of sort.

"And it shall come to pass at that time, that I will search Jerusalem with candles, and punish the men that are settled on their lees; that say in their heart, the LORD will not do good, neither will He do evil." Zephaniah 1:12 (KJV)

May the day never come that the Lord will have to search for people in dark places because they are hiding or refuse to hear the truth. Jesus said that should man fail to speak out that God will raise the rocks to bring Glory to Him. I believe the last few years we have been blessed to see the archeological finds that are being dug up. Let's look at them real close for what they are. These finds are rocks that are being dug up to testify to the things of God! We must become a walking testimony in doing the work of the Lord!

I am certain that there are those that believe that asking for forgiveness is enough even though they continue on in rebellion. The meaning of repentance is a turning away from. We cannot repent and ride on cheap grace as a way when God's Word is clear about what needs to happen in our lives. Not answering God does not stop the commitment; it intensifies the call and the path you will certainly walk.

Many called ministers have settled into a mold, not wanting to deviate for a number of reasons. I am not any different than the next guy! I would love to know that I have a good safe and secure income to support my family. We would love to have a place that we can call home and sit back in the privacy of that home from time to time. There are many things, if we denied what God wanted us to do, we could strive towards but there would be no joy in them. We have churches that are settled and cannot move from where they are. This doesn't make them bad places. They are doing a work for God. They are not the ones that are called to do what you may have been called to do. Many a Pastor gets frustrated over the non-movement within a church and they decide on their own which way to go. (Proverbs 3:5) Some churches get shaken from time to time but that is all God's work and not mans'. If your calling is to church planting, pray and ensure that it is the Lord telling you to go forth and take care of that work for Him. The joys are great and the experience will never be matched, I don't believe. If you are one of the angry Pastors, frustrated with where the church is at today, please don't believe that your quest into church planting is the answer. Your thought pattern, if your own, will surely cause you to have some severe struggles. The problems in an older established church are no more and perhaps less than in a new plant. There is no change in how God or the devil works in either area. Stay secure in the arms of God and follow Him not matter what!

Being totally sold out, ready to move beyond the norm and letting God handle all things is what is going to get you through. (Matthew 6:19-21) But! But what! I have a family to take care of, I have personal obligations, and I have many things that must be dealt with! My brothers and Sisters, may I remind you, we faced the same issues and you are not alone in those issues now says God's word. (1Peter 4:12-19) I must share with you something the Lord spoke to me as I argued with Him over going into church planting. I have already said that we are a family, therefore, no money, or actually a small VA pension of $102.00 a month; being told to go spark some theological debate with God! What about my family and what about my pay? God you know what your word says! This is not at all possible! The words of the Lord still ring loud in my ears just like the day He said them, don't you know that I love your family even more than you do? How can one respond to that? Tough! Yes! God is the one that will get us through!

CHAPTER TWO

The Gifts of God - Romans 12

Romans 12: *"I BESEECH you therefore, brethren, by the mercies of God, that ye present your bodies a living sacrifice, holy, acceptable unto God, which is your reasonable service."*

God has a way of building His church! There have been times within the ministry that I was sure that God was making a mistake in the direction He told me to take. There was one time that we had another minister in the church that was creating some problems within the body. I had prayed and prayed about the situation. The Lord gave me a scripture to preach from. (I will take more about it later) I begged the Lord not to have me preach that message! I lay prostrate on the floor of the little church location for about three hours weeping and seeking the Lord's direction. After several hours, I felt a hand touch me and a gentle voice spoke and ask me was I finished with my temper tantrum? What! I was praying, I thought, but God saw it as rebellion against Him (Isaiah 45:9). He had told me to preach the message He gave me. That night, as I drifted off to sleep, the Lord woke me up with a knock on the door! (Job 33:14-16). Nobody heard this knock! We had a dog that barked at everything and he was sleeping away. At first, I thought I was just hearing things but, as I drifted back off to sleep, it happened again! This time I sat up and asked the Lord what He wanted me to see. I was standing in a room, bright and pure white with books all around and one solitary table in the room. It was God and I standing in this office having a discussion. You see, I had resolved how I could preach the message the Lord had given me without hurting any feelings. Unfortunately, God wasn't happy with my solution and decided to speak to me again! He walked over to a shelf and removed a book; they were all blue bound books with solid white covers and backs. This particular book had this minister's name on it and the words, "Office of God." God took this book and opened it with angry motions. He told me He had this against the man and this against him and this against him as He flipped through the pages. I begged the Lord; let me go talk to Him Lord! No! I have spoken to him, you have spoken to him, and now is the time you speak the message I have given you. The discussion continued as I told the Lord about how this man loved us and He answered, by asking, "Are you sure?" I told Him about how this man loves Him and the Lord returned with

"You think so!" I told Him the man loves the church and the Lord responded with, "You believe that?" Then He spoke to me and told me to preach what He said or He would be mad at me just like that. I argued again about what it would do to the church and the Lord simply reminded me, It IS HIS church!

The next morning, before service, another minister called me with a word from God telling me that I was doing exactly what God wanted done. This minister was in Mexico and had no knowledge of what was happening in central Texas.

I say this to say, God is still working through His gifts that He gives, as He desires. He begins the 12th chapter of Romans with what it is we must do. He says we are to present our bodies a living sacrifice, holy, acceptable unto God, which is your reasonable service. He goes on to say that we are not to be conformed to the things of this world but be transformed by the renewing of your mind, that you may prove what is good, and acceptable, and perfect will of God (Romans 12:1-3). We must be willing to do the things the Lord leads us to do even through the difficult times. God will help us to see our way through. The means and channels He uses are up to Him and Him alone.

This transformation that God speaks about is the avenue to the power that allows God to bring about change in us and throughout the world. Our willingness to let God be God in all things through revelation knowledge from His Spirit allows us to discern those things that are from Him. God says that if it is of Him it will stand and if it is not, it will surely fall. We must learn to trust Him as we grow through things.

I can look back to a political election back in the late 1980's or early 90's. I am not sure of the dates right off. I will not disclose the names and will be leaving out some information that can lead to the tracking of this story for the benefit of our dear friends. I was helping a late politician's widow as she was running for her deceased husband's political office. She had opted not to run for his office immediately after his death for a number of reasons. Her husband was killed in a tragic accident. He had left home that night to a sporting event but the news came later that evening of his accident. His widow shared with me about her visit to the accident site. She said he was wearing a light blue suit that night with a dark blue shirt. The collar and shirts cuffs showed up as bright edges in his apparel. As she was speaking to the Lord at the accident sight, a butterfly came over and gently landed on her arm. It was a light blue butterfly with dark blue outline around it. She said she knew immediately that her husband's transformation had been completed and he was sitting at the feet of our Savior and Lord Jesus the Christ. The epitaph on his tombstone reads, "Mission Accomplished, Gone Home!" Transformation was complete for him.

As we see new churches being planted, we are hearing the cries of rebellion from those that have set stagnant for many years. There are those that believe that God is not still doing the very things He did from the beginning. There are those that have stopped their transformation to be conformed to the ways of the world. There are those that will stop anything that would cause the church to be different for fear of the church's reputation. When we compromise with the things of this world and stop standing on the word of God, we are damaging the reputation of the church.

The church is made of many members but yet one body (Romans 12:4-5). Wow! What a concept! God has placed all kinds of things within our midst, if we should only take hold of them. They are given to us according to the grace of God to be used for Him and the church, not to be separated. We find prophesy within the beginning of the list in Romans 12. What can we do with prophesy that will satisfy the Lord? The other thing He says about prophecy is, we prophesy by the proportion of faith we have! What! Speak it and it shall happen! No way! This is trying to tell God what to do! We are in uncharted territory here for some folks. We are told in the Word of the Lord that we are to declare a thing and it shall be established this day. What are we doing? One that is walking in the conformity of worldly religion would get upset over these things. One that is in the stage of transformation will watch the glory of God being revealed through His hand and His people. This gift deals with the ability to read God's word and interpret it and deliver a message from it. It is not limited to this however and is used to help people and glorify God.

While we were in Texas, I had visited with a church leader some 700 miles away from us, for about 15 minutes one day. The Lord spoke to me about him some 6 months later. He told me to pray for the man or he would not be in the position of leadership he was in much longer. I called the man, after praying for him. He was on vacation. I made several other attempts to talk with him but with no results. I had his email address, so I sent him an e-mail! Within 15 minutes I received a message back wanting to know how I knew what was going on because no one knew outside of his family. Spiritual fortune telling is what people want to call this from time to time. There is nothing that is fortune telling related in a revelation from God. This was word knowledge or the knowledge of the past and present.

What about the area of ministry? I believe we all have a place to work within the body of the church. We cannot all be arms, legs or heads, but we can all work. Sometimes we have those within the church that resemble the intestines, they just grumble every once in a while, but most oftentimes help things to move regularly. God has a job for everyone!

He speaks of teachers within this scripture. There are always needs for teachers within the church for Sunday school or Discipleship Training. There are many ways we can teach outside of the walls of the church. Some of the ministry of teaching is sharing your duties with someone else that they may learn how to accomplish what the Lord has you doing. We oftentimes become territorial and try not to disclose how we do things for job security and control. Our first mission to teach is linked to the great commission in making disciples (Matthew 28:19-20). Somehow, we come to believe that the children in our churches are the church of tomorrow. I am not sure how all that got started but, they certainly are the church of what's happening now and the leaders of tomorrow. They must be led and taught by the leaders today and the leaders today must be willing to relinquish those positions tomorrow.

The gift of Exhortation is not supposed to be a gift that causes us to speak at a level that no one can understand but calls for simplicity in relating God's Holy Word to your life and the lives of others. When things are kept simple, it will allow people to understand quicker and more fully what the message would mean. The key thing to reaching the people will be making the message relevant to them in the daily lives. God is the only one that can do that through His messengers.

As a young minister, my teaching was that there were three places that messages for the church will come from. The three means were, Inspiration, observation and liturgical calendars. As the Lord began to reveal things about the church to me, His inspiration/revelation began to merge into my observations and even the liturgical calendar fell in line. God is fully aware of what is going on and will speak the words when, where and how He wants them delivered. God wants His people to know where He stands and where they stand with Him!

If we recall, when the Israelites came out of captivity, the Hebrew language was almost lost. The Priest read the scrolls and the Levites caused them to understand what was contained therein (Nehemiah 8:5-8).

Although we are in a ruler's area of giftedness while planting a church, it is wise to remember the real ruler is God! God does not beat us up and call us names to get us to do anything. God leads us through gentleness and love. When we get out of line, then He will do those things required to get us back into the fold. I recall a trip we made into Mexico in 2002. As we were going down the straightest road I have ever seen, we saw a heard of goats being whipped by the herder and the dogs were really working to keep them in line. They ran all over the area trying to keep things in some fashion of order. You could see the herder yelling at his goats. As we went further down the road, the Lord took my attention to a shepherd that was leading his sheep through a field. He was leading and the sheep were right behind him. The sheep dogs were there but they were just walking along beside the sheep. There was peace and unity in the midst of the flock. The Lord spoke to me and told me, you have just seen the difference between a shepherd and goat herder. Those sheep probably didn't always act that way and took some training. The church plants will require extensive training that only the Lord can bring about through His word. God has inspired books that will aid in your work for the Lord. God's word must be paramount and not compromised. It will require much work and many sleepless nights.

There are many people that have been hurt through churches today. They are hurt from families and life's situations. We must show that loving mercy that only God can give as people begin to enter into the doors. We must be cautious to not get into the trap of building a church based on personal anger brought in from others. This will certainly create more problems than you would want. Jesus said to be wise as a serpent and gentle as a dove. Be wise in showing mercy.

As a church, we must learn to love unconditionally. There can be no discrimination as to who comes to church and how they dress. We must love them regardless. There are many things we find offensive and I can assure you that God sees much offensive too! I believe we are to strive to reach a point that God doesn't see our lack of love for others as a problem (Matthew 5:48).

We have seen churches that want to get things done as they begin. There has been much successes made, and many failures, because of the business tactics of man. We once lost a piece of property that was donated to a work because the man went back on his word and the shortcuts we took in the paperwork left us no place to go with the land deal. It was my lack of business sense that caused that. I was the one that fell short but learned a valuable lesson. We prayed for the Lord to provide and when He did, we dropped the ball.

God later provided another piece of property. (Matthew 18:19)

We have seen God deliver on His promises time and again to watch the leadership of His church not pick up the ball and run. We must, as instructed, adhere to the laws of the land and take care of the legal matters involving the church. When God provides the land, we must move in making it sure in the eyes of the law. We work backwards sometimes in these areas. We pray and worry about what God is doing about providing what we are praying for and when it is given, all interest is dropped and the business is not dealt with accordingly. Instill in your plant the necessity to take care of this business. God will have someone there to help you through. If that gift is not yet apparent, that responsibility lands on the church planter and no one else. Remember the Levites were responsible for the things of the temple.

We must remain committed to God as we move forward. Sometimes it is hard when you are first getting started. Many times, there is a lack of musicians and a lack of people's commitment. Be faithful and stand firm. We had the little plant in Texas and there was nothing but a tape recorder for our music. We prayed for a piano player or someone with musical talent. One Sunday, after morning worship, the Lord sent us a minister that had been absent from the ministry to see us. He wanted to know if he could bring his praise band up to the church and become a part of us! He asked me to meet him later at the building but I just handed him a key! The man was an answer to prayer and that band brought some needed life to the work. God used this man and his worship ministry during our time there. God blessed him by placing him in the Pastoral ministry there as we left.

There are many other gifts the Lord equips His people with in doing His work. We are to encourage one another as we labor for the Lord. Some people are around for the purpose of encouraging people to move on toward the forward mark while yet another is seeking to reach a balance of not pushing or lagging behind through the exercise of patience.

Pray for the churches in the areas around you. Pray they get so full they cannot contain all the people and they will need to go into a building program. Ask the Lord to Bless them even though there will be many that will stand against what you are doing. We have had other Pastors preach against the work the Lord was doing through us from their church pulpits as we prayed for them

God will use all these gifts in the building of His work. We will look more into the other gifts as we move towards the next chapter.

CHAPTER THREE

Gifts of the Holy Spirit - 1 Corinthians 12-14

It is sad to say that this is the most disputed area of the church today! I was raised in another denomination and there was probably no one that could be as cold to these gifts as I was, until! I was speaking to the Lord one day in respect to the Gifts of the Spirit. I asked Him, Lord, why do you not use these gifts in your church anymore? Why are they gone? If you don't ever change Lord, what happened? I thought these were good questions. Maybe I even thought that I was putting God on the spot. Hey God, you don't change but this stuff, well, it is said doesn't exist anymore. The Lord spoke to me and told me, Randy, I never quit giving gifts, the Holy Spirit never quit giving gifts and Jesus never quit calling Apostles and Prophets. What! He hasn't changed! God placed their absence from the church right square in the laps of us. He said the reason we do not see these gifts exercised anymore is because people have stopped them and denied them from existence in their religious beliefs (2 Timothy 3:1-9). Sometimes it is easier to turn a deaf ear to something that might cause a disruption in the norm. I know you have seen people turn from something and pretend it never happened as opposed to taking a stand.

These gifts are given as the Holy Spirit apportions them (1 Corinthians 12:11). They are not given for show and they are not given to bring glory to anyone in the church but God. God does not need to show off in front of people, He's God!

We find those with us that can look into the Word and come up with instantaneous Divine revelation on a scripture. God will fill their mouth with the words to speak when the time comes. I wrote earlier about the man that I had e-mailed about his situation. As I e-mailed a response to his questions, I referred him to the scriptures here about the gift of word knowledge. This can be a scary thing when someone walks up to you and tells you things the Lord is revealing about you.

We were Pastoring a church once where the Lord spoke to me about a man that came to the church. He had not established a firm relationship with God and was seeking to get beyond some things. The Lord had things for him to do in the future. We went to his home and asked him could we share some things with him. I shared what the Lord told me about him and allowed him to speak frankly about the matters. He accepted Jesus as Lord and Savior that night! (His family told us, after we left, he could not even hold on to a measuring spoon for coffee. All he could say was God had snitched on him.) ☺ About two weeks later, the Lord gave me a vision about the man again. This time I was pulling barbed wired out of the man's teeth with a pair of pliers. I got to the last barb and it would not come out. The Lord told me to cut it off. The message, there was a thorn in the flesh that would probably never be removed but it had to be stopped. It is tough to deliver some messages when God reveals things. When you are sure it is God, you must discern what to do with the message whether to deliver or pray about the message. This gift has been helpful in church planting and Pastoral work.

We went to a church in central Texas preaching in view of a call. The night before we went the Lord gave me some knowledge about a man within that church that needed some healing. He had some neck problems and he couldn't turn his head from side to side. As we met the man in McDonalds the next morning, I began to tell him about the vision I had. (I knew it was he.) I told him about what the Lord had shown me, and then I asked him, you don't know who that would be, do you? The man just about yelled as he said, "that's me!" We had service and prayed for him after the service as the Lord had spoken and the man, to this day remembers the day the Lord healed his neck and back problems! Praise the Lord!

When the Holy Spirit tells us to do something for Him, the provisions are made to accomplish the mission. Whoops! I got carried away and told you about the gift of healing before I got down to it. This is a gift that God uses in His choosing but is still alive and well. We do not claim to be anything or anyone other than a servant of God's and He has been faithful in answering our prayers for healing of many.

For those that are of the belief that Gifts of the Spirit are not still alive, we run into a sticky point as we approach the gift of prophesy once again. It is an overlap of a gift. The gift of prophecy is given by God, and here we find it through the Holy Spirit. If a gift were dead in one area, certainly there would be no need for it at all. What about working of miracles? We see a miracle every time a person in drawn to the Lord! That is the true miracle that is the most important. While we were in Mexico, we saw God perform miracle after miracle. It was during the last service, where an Evangelist preached; that the Lord spoke to me about praying for two souls He was trying to reach. Being the pious Pastor that I can sometimes be, I bowed my head and began to pray. The Lord got firm in His insistence for me to pray. He told me to get down at that first pew, on my knees and cry out for those two lost souls, with agony, like Jesus cried out for mine in the garden. I don't know how long I was down there crying out to Him when He told me to get up. The long and short was, two souls were brought to the Lord that night and God reminded me that there is no miracle or anything as important to Him as the redemption of the human soul. But there are other miracles God does use His people to perform for Him. But in the area of miracles, the big difference is the element of time required for healing is removed and the healing takes place instantly. God can do anything He wants to do and we have seen Him do much in this area.

The gift that it seems like everybody sitting in a church pew claims to have is the gift of discernment. It is the most claimed gift but probably the least possessed when the real truth bears out. God says that all things are spiritually discerned but cannot be done so until you have received the Spirit of God (1 Corinthians 2:14). There are a lot of lost people within the pews of our churches today that believe they have God figured out. I learned that if it makes sense, it probably is not God working at all. God does things much different than mankind does them. This gift cannot be received except through the regenerated soul of the believer and God dwelling in them. Many who claim to have this gift are not showing the fruits of God's children and yet are claiming to know God's ways. Beware of the fruit they bear! It is the true revelation of good and evil.

Are these gifts alive today? God says, He is the Lord God and He does not change! (Malachi 3:6) Yes, these gifts are alive. I can get this far down the list ok, but I got to a sticking point. I struggled with the issue of speaking in tongues and interpretation. I tried for years to fit this into the box I wanted it in. I couldn't seem to get it to fit anywhere that it could be contained. I preached with tiptoe type steps about this subject for a while and even tried to avoid it. One Sunday night, during the Praise and Worship part of the service, a glory cloud showed up in the sanctuary and the Glory of God fell! The Lord spoke to me and told me to pay attention; He was going to show me something. It became peacefully quiet and a man stood and delivered a message in some language, sounding to me as Aramaic (1 Corinthians 14:30-33). I was in a panic, as to what was going on as this was happening! What do I do? The Lord said to sit still, it was He. I looked and the Guitar player was in a trance, the bass player was on his knees in tears and the Lord spoke to me what was being said. The Guitar player stepped up to the microphone and interpreted the utterance into English. We went straight back into worship with a tempo that I have not seen since. It was indeed an awesome experience. The next morning the guitar player came to the house and asked me what had been said. He didn't even know what he had spoken for the Lord. The following Monday night it happened again during a Hispanic service, involving all different people with Cheryl being the only person in common at the two services. Yes, God still speaks to His people through His people! We are told that these gifts are used to edify the Body of Christ. We cannot try to use them for our own glory or we will surely fail. God says these gifts will be here until the Perfect comes (1 Corinthians 13:9-10). I believe we can all come to the common ground that the only perfect is Christ and that since this was written after the death and resurrection of Christ, it has to be referring to His return to redeem His church.

This takes us into the gifts listed in chapter 13 of 1 Corinthians. We find Faith, Hope and Love listed and the Lord tells us the greatest of all these is Love.

Everything else will pass away but Love shall endure forever. There will be no need for these gifts upon the return of Christ as He is the fulfillment of them all. The reason behind the endurance of Love is that God is Love and He is Everlasting to Everlasting (Revelation 22:13).

Not all people have all these gifts of the Holy Spirit, in fact there are probably many that don't and few that do. We are simply vessels or conduits in using any of these gifts and are not of any use at all if we try them by ourselves. They are here to edify the whole body that believers might grow in faith and that unbelievers may come to a point of belief through these works.

I would send forth a word of caution to those that have questions about any of these gifts and the exercise in them. God will show you His work verses any false work that may be being done. Hone in on the spiritual gift of prophecy as the Lord says (1 Corinthians 14:1). Know His Word and you will be able to discern the truth from the false. The only way you can really know the Word is to be in a relationship with God, through Christ that is intimate. I can assure you, you would understand more fully the writings in this book and any other book, if you knew the heartbeat of the author. He says the works of the flesh are obvious. He is a God of order. He also says that the prophet controls the spirit that is in him. People who create controversy through the use of these gifts are simply out of the will of God.

CHAPTER FOUR

Gifts of Christ or 5-Fold Ministry - Ephesians 4:11

Ephesians 4:11-12: *"And he gave some, apostles; and some, prophets; and some, evangelists; and some, pastors and teachers; For the perfecting of the saints, for the work of the ministry, for the edifying of the body of Christ:"*

In the modern church, we have adopted the theology that God no longer uses the Apostle or the Prophet in a calling. These are probably the most disputed areas of the ministry. You have the Apostles, the Prophets, the Evangelists, the Pastors and the Teachers encompassed in what Jesus uses within His church. Once again, we stand and deny that these callings exist while standing before the Lord and telling Him that we know He doesn't change. How can we become stable in our relationship with God without believing the Bible as the absolute truth from God and about God? The Word says that a double-minded man is unstable in all his ways (James 1:8). We are at an impasse. Does Jesus still call Apostles and Prophets or are we now working in a 3-fold ministry where the Pastor has been handed all the other responsibility? In my search of the Word of God, I have not seen any sign that the torch was passed and offices called within the church were deleted. It is written that:

"Now therefore ye are no more strangers and foreigners, but fellow citizens with the saints, and of the household of God; and are built upon the foundation of the apostles and prophets, Jesus Christ himself being the chief cornerstone;" Ephesians 2:19-20 (KJV)

The word of God makes it plain that churches are founded through an organized principle, approved through Him and that the five-fold ministry is still alive and doing well. Without the role of Apostles and Prophets, there would surely be no church planters or even missionaries to other places.

Although I will receive some denominational fire for some things contained in this book, I can only attest to those things the Lord has revealed to me. Some things are not popular to talk about within the religious structure today. The sad thing is, we are shutting God down in the religious circles today to where He is not able to do His work through us. I am of the firm understanding that, where it applies to the 5-fold ministry, these gifts are not only gifts but are actual job assignments by Jesus for us to serve Him. People baulk when someone uses the title Apostle but, what is the difference in that and church bodies not wanting to call their minister Pastor? To me, it is a way to drag God's called to a level where the people are and treat them as they treat all others. In fact, there are many churches that will treat a thief with better treatment than they do their sent minister. Does this sound familiar as we look back to the crucifixion of Christ? (Luke 23:18-19)

We have, in our society belittled the people that God has called to serve Him and taken away their positions in the name of harmony. I can assure you, when a church no longer calls their Pastor, "Pastor"; they are trying to bring that person down to their level of thinking.

Apostles are those that are called to forsake all they have and follow Christ in a new direction. Sometimes it is leaving the security of a warm house and a good income. There are many sacrifices that we are called to make but the Apostle and prophet are the ones that seem to be tasked to surrender more (Luke 9:3). This goes back to my earlier statement about God only uses those that have been tried and proven through the furnace of affliction. They are the ones that seem to be called to a life of poverty for a season. As one person said about us, they are just living off the fat of the land.

I can assure you, in central Texas, the land wasn't very fat but God can do everything!

Unfortunately, if we had a legalist in the religious area today, the Apostle would probably be the office that God called to be that way. This is the calling that requires that structure be developed and that government of the church be placed, according to the vision of God. The real issues are not the Apostles but the teachings we have had over the years that we own the church and can do what we want to do. Under Ecclesiastical Government, the church can be successful but once the people begin to pervert this government through their personal wants, it creates a place of contention. The Apostle gets called a dictator at times while trying to get God's work done. Is it any wonder most planters try to get into a place where older believers do not get involved because their experiences can hinder the work? As we support the work of the Lord, ultimately, we support the work of the Apostle. God sent them to get the church started! (Romans 10:14-15) It is more than likely they who have made all the sacrifices that need to be made in getting started. Apostles seem to have a special connection to God that resembles that of Joshua. It seems they can always hear the voice of God as they work and meditate.

Prophets are still alive and well today. We have seen them in action. There is a close friend that we had put in our lives while we were in Texas. Our bond is so close that to this day, when he prays for us or we pray for him, we know it. This brother was placed under the covering of our ministry some three years ago. He is very plain and meets the descriptions of a prophet. He is likeable to us and very serious in his work. There is nothing that he doesn't talk to the Lord about and he fears no evil as he walks. He goes where the Lord sends him and he gave up virtually everything to follow God. Not many of us can actually say we gave up millions to follow the Lord like this man is capable of saying. I would like to say, He has never made mention of what sacrifice he made to serve God. He rejoices in the way God uses him. He carries good messages and messages of encouragement for ministers. He helps them in times of spiritual battles. This guy is explosive. What makes him this way? His obedience and willingness to do God's work is what makes him the way he is. He is nobody in the spectrum of things. The people in his hometown have rejected him as being off his rocker. This man is a walking example that God still uses prophets to get His work done. A prophet's responsibility is to carry a message to wherever it is to go both inside and outside of the church. They cannot force someone to hear the message and receive it, all they can do is speak it and their job is finished. There is no telling how many of these people the Lord has out working for Him that folks are calling nuts.

The Evangelist is called to do one thing, spread the Gospel message of Christ and the Salvation afforded through Him and Him alone. The evangelist is responsible to the Pastor of the church he or she is in. It is a subordinate ministry yet outside the church, it stands alone. No minister in their right mind would ever try to hinder an evangelistic ministry but would serve to promote them and help them to get places where they can do God's work. This ministry operates predominately outside of the church.

The Pastor is the person in the middle. As a church planter, you see the role of the Pastor transform. Once you end up doing that job, you will see the way the five-fold ministry should serve together as designed to edify the body of Christ. The prophet and the apostle, once their work is done, should they remain in the church, work in unison with the leadership of the Pastor. The Pastor will become responsible for the work once God has established one for the work (Jeremiah 3:15). This shouldn't happen for a while after the plant takes place.

Teachers are Christ called too! They need to be called so they can deal with their areas of responsibility. I am always saying that I wasn't called to talk to the youth because my tolerance would be too thin. These teachers all have a special job to do in helping people to grow into a better, more mature Christian. Their duties are only limited by imagination.

The callings of these positions are to equip the saints, to edify the body of Christ (Ephesians 4:12). All we do, no matter the position, is to bring Glory to God.

As the Lord sends in people to the new work, He will begin to identify them and you will be able to see God putting things together. Things are not always what they appear to be as we see them developing. Stay in prayer.

At one point in a church plant, we had 13 ordained ministers from all over. I found that they could become controversial as they began to differ with the vision the Lord had given us. Stay true to God's vision and He will sort them out. We watched Him take them out two by two until the problems were reduced to nothing. After He took out the last two, I asked the Lord what had just happened. He took me to Jeremiah and began to speak to me about Jeremiah's youth. He was sent into a bunch of prophets that had not been so truthful and they were sent into bondage. Jeremiah was known as the weeping prophet and the Lord revealed that the message was a bitter one but the position of a young man chosen to go against seasoned and known people was one of humility for Jeremiah. So was the situation as we grew through the appearance and disappearance of all these people that had been proclaiming something other than what the Lord wanted to be heard. These controversies can be expected within the first year and will tax you hard. God will carry you through it.

A man once told me, "God will never place you where His grace won't sustain you until the job is done." These are some great words of wisdom from a good man of God.

As this is the close of three chapters on the gifts, I would like to emphasize that all gifts may not be present in all churches and you may never experience some of them in your lifetime as I may not experience some of them in my lifetime or ever again. I just praise God for what He has allowed us to do for Him thus far. All of the gifts given will help us to grow in Christ through their proper uses!

CHAPTER FIVE

Being Genuine - Mark 11:11-22

Mark 11:22; *"And Jesus answering saith unto them, 'Have faith in God"*

For years I struggled with the account of the cursing of the fig tree by Jesus. I could not buy in on the theology that this was a non-productive person that was supposedly serving the Lord. It was not until we had been in church planting for a while that this was beginning to make some sense to me. One morning while I was in prayer, I asked the Lord about the fig tree and what all this really meant. Now, as we look into this account of the tree being cursed, we have it broken down for us in several Bibles beginning in verse 12. God had me read the scripture from verse 12 and down to verse 22. It still didn't make sense. It just appeared that Jesus was on a rampage of anger after a bad night of sleep. Then the Lord took me back to verse 11 and showed me that Jesus had been in the Temple the night before and looked around. Jesus saw what was happening there and didn't like it then. He saw the corruption in the House of God and it brought Him great displeasure. The next morning, Jesus, along with His disciples was heading back into Jerusalem for the day when they happed upon the fig tree.

The fig tree represents the people of Israel and the country or governmental structure itself. You see that was why the big impact with the destruction of the Temple in 70 AD. It stood for everything Israel was about. The Priests of the Temple had led the people of Israel and they weren't capable of being productive as God's people. They had become caught up in religious tradition and dogma (Ezekiel 44:10-14).

The Lord Jesus went to the tree, seeing it was in full bloom, to see if it had any fruit on it, knowing it was too early. Jesus knows the growth of everything. He knows who will bear fruit and when. Jesus is the vine and we are the branches. We receive our nourishment from Him and no other. Any other way as an attempt to bear fruit is false (Psalm 1:3). This was the problem that was in the Temple at the time. People were being led through false teachings that were not coming from the wisdom of God but from the wisdom of man.

Oh, how my heart aches when we look around us and see people teaching people how to act like Christians but they are not even in a relationship with

Christ. We can teach people the things to do to fit in as they come to church (Mark 7:8-13). It is extremely easy for us to teach people to give a few dollars or to dress in a new way to attend church as a matter of formality. We should teach people to give, don't get me wrong. One fellow in Texas once told me, Randy, if the Lord's got your heart; He's got your pocket book. This is so true. We should be careful in our teachings to let each person know that Jesus truly loves them and He alone is the source of true growth. It breaks the heart of God to see someone that is in need of some help and a person to lead them to a point of salvation and the person they go to has been in church for a long time but they have no idea how to lead a person to the foot of the cross and help them get into that personal relationship with Christ. These people who have such a relationship will in fact dry up from the roots and die. They simply are not tapped into the living waters that never run dry (John 15:1-2). God loves His people and wants them to come to Him. After we abide in Him, He will allow you to bear fruit in His season.

The fig tree simply represents the product of the Temple and the nation of Israel. They were a product of the Temple, are we? Or are we a Holy Spirit product?

When Jesus comes to visit His Father's House today and finds things that are not in order, He will cleanse those Houses too! (Ezekiel 9:1-11) Jesus went in and found the workers of the Temple dealing as Dove Handlers and Money Changers. They were practicing corruption within the House of God. They had begun to institute many things the Lord did not command. They were in a state that we would refer to in the church today as spiritual adultery. They had become extreme legalists with rules overriding God's Word.

Well, ok Randy, How can this apply to the modern church? Could it be that we too get caught up in doing things our own way as we begin to do church plants? It is easy to get caught up in the norm of things. People from all over will come in and look for programs within the church. There are many churches that are built from programs and man-made loyalties. It first takes a church to be grown before programs can be developed. How can we get caught up in this you might ask? There are things that happen to generate money to take care of the business of the church. Some churches have Bingo and others may have draw down raffles while others have bake sales. These things are sometimes done as an effort to build a church and we forget the focus is to bring Glory to God by leading souls to Him. There are other programs people begin to worship too! There is the requirement to have a school bus or van, we must have many youth activities and we must get a program to draw people in from all age groups. These programs can run us in circles for a long time. It is not bad to have programs within the church. Bake sale and other things that are not immoral or unethical are not bad either. The key thing is, we must not build the church on programs but rather have the church develop the programs that fit the church as it grows. These programs will shift from time to time and many of the programs will come and go. We should be careful that the programs of the church serve the people and the people don't become servants to the programs above God. With this, we should keep God as the main focal point of the work always! (John 12:32) Be careful about letting programs dictate the direction of the church just to keep up with the other churches in town. The fig tree was not cursed for being barren but for the falsity of the profession of being something it wasn't, symbolizing the people and the nation.

Jesus addressed the Scribes and Pharisees later during this same week. He called them hypocrites! He told them that they went all over the sea and land to bring one person unto their selves and they make the person twice the son of perdition as they are. We are not trying to duplicate people as they serve the Lord but get the Good News out and see souls brought to God through Christ. Oh, the glory of watching the transformation of believers!

Jesus was admonishing the people then and reminds us now that the House of the Lord is to be a House of Prayer. We must reverence His place as we come to worship Him. Jesus also said to bring no unclean vessel into the Temple. This is another thing we must be careful about. We must allow people to enter and hear the Good News but the unclean, un-regenerated soul has no place in the leadership of the church. As believers, we must also enter into God's presence pure in heart.

In verse 22, Jesus spoke to His disciples again and told them to have faith and believe in God. We are good at trying to do things for God when all that is required of us is to believe. We work to build churches and see the people come. He says that no man comes to the Father unless the Holy Spirit draws him. There really is nothing we can do that is more effective that fervent prayer for the lost. Jesus spoke in John saying that if He should be lifted up then He will draw all men nigh unto Him. God has placed the very best church growth plan before our very eyes. It doesn't entail spending or raising tons on money. God doesn't want His church to be encumbered with a load of debt! He simply wants us to believe that He will draw them and use us at the same time. When we bear fruit, we are lifting up the name of Jesus. God will send in the provisions to do the work that is going on with us.

It is no accident that the cursing of the fig tree is sandwiched between these two visits to the Temple and the ultimate cleansing of the Temple. God gave a revelation that I believe is as real today as it was then.

As we look back into Luke 2 and the account of the angels appearing to the shepherds as they watched their flocks by night, there is a picture of what God would have His church to look like. We see, as we read that the Angels came and the singing was heard from the heavens. These angels were worshipping the Savior that was born that day. The modern church should be singing and praising God all the time! When we do this, we see the rest of the picture as God says, the Glory of

God shown round about them. Brothers and Sisters, when we get to doing the things the way God wants them to be done, we get to where we can get our feet off the ground in praising Him, our knees on the ground when it comes to worship, and our face on the floor in prayer we will in fact see the Glory of the Lord shine round about the work. What a great feeling it is when all of this happens!

As we planted a church in central Texas, we had a severe storm go through the area. Once the storm was over, there was not one but two rainbows that crossed over the town. It was an amazing thing to see. Cheryl and I were amazed to see two rainbows at the same time in the same area of the sky. The next morning, a lady brought to us a picture of one of the rainbows taken from a perspective she could see. The beginning of the rainbow appeared to be coming right out of the very building from which we had the church meetings. What beauty to behold!

We sometimes have a little difficulty in believing that God will bring people to where He is located. We were in the middle of a Big Tent Revival in Texas. One morning a man showed up from 85 miles away. I asked him how he had heard about us and his response was that he didn't know we were there but the Lord brought him right to us. God's Holy Spirit drew this man! This has happened on more occasions than we can count. God's word and His promises are all we can stand on and know they will be exactly as God said they would be and will continue to be.

So, what do we do to accomplish the things that God would have us to do? We have found there is never enough prayer. I don't care how much you pray; you must pray some more. The work must be grounded on the Doctrine of Christ through God's Word and that alone. We will see the love grow as the knowledge of God's word increases (2 Peter 1:5-8). The more we learn about the Love of God, the more we realize it is all about God and His love for us, and nothing more. We must help to build a solid Biblical foundation as we go and provide proper Biblical spiritual guidance. When we do these things, Jesus will be lifted up! My prayer is that no rock will have to be dug up to praise the Lord on my account. May I always shout Glory and Honor to the Lamb that was slain!

CHAPTER SIX

Carnality in the Church - Numbers 12

Numbers 12:1-2; "*And Miriam and Aaron spake against Moses because of the Ethiopian woman whom he had married; for he had married and Ethiopian woman. And they said, Hath the Lord indeed spoken only by Moses? Hath he not spoken also by us? And the Lord heard it.*"

As we look into the Old Testament writings, we find a small squabble about power within the organizational structure. God had selected Moses to speak directly to and through to His people. While they were out of the will of God, God referred to them as Moses' people. We see a position of jealousy coming into play. There was murmuring in the camp from Aaron and Miriam. They were upset about something. This sounds a lot like what we have to deal with as church planters. There is someone that is going to come in and begin to tell you what the Lord is saying. I am not saying that God doesn't speak to them. This whole rumor started out as a smoke screen against Moses. Moses had married a Cushite woman (Numbers 12:1-2). This was an interracial marriage. His brother and sister began a revolt around the camp. They got people to talking about Moses, trying to demean his position. They had used worldly things to try to change the focus of things. God says that Moses was "meek". This is a word that has been twisted and turned to mean that we should come to a position of compromise. There are churches full of compromise! God isn't looking for more of what already exists! God wants a genuine church centered on His Word and His Grace towards all people. It is not a free rodeo ride that we can get on and enjoy. Being a Christian entails a lifelong commitment to service and standing on the promises of God. God had told Moses what was going on, where He was leading them and Moses simply stood on those things knowing God is indeed God. This is the approach we should take as we encounter challenges in the ministry as we move forward in faith. Being meek does not at all mean being weak but being strong on the word of God and not wavering, sticking to the path God places you on.

Moses' brother and sister were summoned to the Tabernacle to the first big tent revival ever. God met them at the door of the tent and spoke with them. He issued a stern warning to them. He told them that if there is a prophet among you, I will speak to them in dreams and visions but it wasn't so with Moses. God specifically stated that He would speak to Moses face to face, so that he could understand Him. Moses had a direct line to the Lord. Moses was the chosen leader, by the Lord, and that was the respect that God gave to him and required of His people in return.

I remember one night after prayer meeting; we were in the back of the church discussing things that needed to be done in the church. We had a person telling me that we needed to abandon certain plans the church had a vision for. They wanted to pull back all they were doing and center directly within the church and its four walls. That wasn't what the Lord was leading us to do. I told him that the Lord had told me certain things, which we discussed, and he returned with a loud tone, how would you know that? Well, I told him, it was quite simple, the Lord told me these things. That ended the discussion. God will reveal things to you that only you will know. It is your position to share that vision and watch God lead the way as you pray. I am not saying that others will not eventually come in with ways to reach that vision that will not match up with your thought pattern. The approach may be different but the vision the same in many cases.

We find Moses and his brother and sister at the tent. Miriam was stricken with leprosy and banished from the camp. That was her punishment which certainly meant death for her. God has issued a death sentence on to Moses' sister for her behavior. He got right to the root of the problem in dealing with this situation. God always knows where the source of the problem comes from and sometimes, we, as people, miss the exact place of origin. Aaron appealed to Moses and Moses pled to God for Miriam. God left her out of the camp for seven days but did not move the camp. Sometimes, we find ourselves standing on the outside of the camp and God stands in wait for us to get back in so He can move His kingdom on earth further towards the promised land.

Leprosy is a Biblical disease that causes separation. It touches all the senses of the human body. It will cause you to not feel, then later not smell or taste, eventually it will get your eyes and then into your hearing. Those that are trying to hinder the progress of God's work may be stricken with spiritual leprosy. They will reach a place where all they can feel is what they want to feel, all they can see is what they lust for, all they can hear are those things which please them, and all they can smell is odorless because they can no longer smell the stench of the devil in their nostrils. People no longer have the thirst for righteousness just the need to speak hurtful things against what the Lord is trying to do. When you see this happening the church planter becomes the ready target. No senses equal spiritual death or separation from God until intercession or repentance is made. It is easier to get placed into a place of banishment than what we would ever care to believe.

God's judgment falls on some people every day as they walk the face of the earth. It is sad to see that these things happen however, it is from a different prospective, encouraging that we have a God who is committed to do the things He has told us He would do as He paves the way.

There will be those that will create problems but God will handle them. You don't even have to say a word to anyone but Him. He knew before you did. I once got upset with a man for his comments in the church about scaring people into salvation. I listened to him yell at me for about an hour and finally just told him to go home and he should find another church. God chastised me and told me to go and make amends with him. I did and the man came back to the church. He didn't stay long, but when he left, the Lord told me I had done my part. It was during that time I learned that God takes people out when He gets ready. It is not up to me to separate the wheat and the tares for Him. It is merely my duty and calling to preach to all people the same. The separation of the wheat and the tares and the sheep from the goats is an ongoing process that will culminate at the rapture of the church.

Many times, I have seen the Lord sit still until someone that is essential to the work returns home from a wandering experience. I believe we all spend times in the wilderness at one time or another. Just be encouraged that God is the one leading you as you plant churches and He is the one that will make the crocked places straight and break down the gates (Isaiah 45:1-3). He has the way already paved. All we have to do is get aboard the Highway of Holiness and be on the fast track to His glory (Isaiah 35:8). The Bible says that He directs the footsteps of the righteous. There is another scripture in the Psalms where the Psalmist wrote the He is a lamp unto our feet and a light unto our path. There have been long periods of time that the Lord would only let me see one step at a time. Had He allowed me to see the pathway He had us on, I surly would have ran from the way He wanted me to walk. Never in my lifetime could we have ever imagined planting one church let alone 4 and a distribution warehouse in 20 months with no money. Had God told me these things from the beginning, surly He would have had a fight with me going, like He didn't already! It was a great walk looking back from this side!

CHAPTER SEVEN

Selecting Leaders - Acts 6

Acts 6:3-4; "*Wherefore, brethren, look ye out among you seven men of honest report, full of the Holy Ghost and wisdom, whom we may appoint over this business But we will give ourselves continually to prayer, and to the ministry of the word.*"

One of the things that we have seen in church planting is the placing leaders within the church to early. There are some key things that the Lord speaks to us about in this area. He instructs us to know those that labor among us. We should be fully aware of people's character before placing them in office. If people are different in church than they are at work and at home, chances are the true person will come out and it will not be good for the work of the ministry. The only people that can be consistent in their behavior are those that are sold out to God in all they do. Yes, they will have times that emotions will run away from them and they will say things that they shouldn't but, that doesn't mean they are not good for the church. I know many church leaders that you can walk up on at work and you would be surprised to find out they went to church at all. Beware of these people. They are still in the flesh and can only see and do business in the flesh. Finding Biblically qualified leaders is a time-consuming process. Paul wrote to young Timothy and told him to lay hands on no man suddenly. There are some strong payments that will be required because of this. Just because someone has been in church for thirty years is not a reason to make that person a leader. I know of people that have been to church for 50 years and finally accepted Christ as their personal Savior and they have served in leadership positions for most of those 50 years. How many ministries do you think these people affected and how much of it was adverse or could have been? Do you think they were ever instrumental in destroying an individuals' life in the ministry? What would your responsibility be for disobeying the Word of God? A church will affect the lives of countless people during its existence and we should do all things with due diligence in selecting proper leaders. The church's effect should always be positive. These people will more than likely be there when you leave and they will be a direct reflection on you and your leadership.

When the first Deacons were placed into the church, there were thousands of people within the church. They were elected to be table waiters. They were to be servants and no more. They were to serve the people at the direction of the Pastor. They were an extension of the Pastor's ministry that would prove to be indispensable later. These folks have a position that is not one to be envied in the church today. They catch all the flack and must be ready to take a stand on the Word of God and work with the Pastor at all times. They are not however intended to be spiritual leaders in a church. I am not trying to be hard on Deacons! I am pointing out that their responsibility has been turned into a form of authority over the years through controlling and manipulation tactics that have caused many a minister trouble. The first Deacons were selected because they were born again believers; filled with the Holy Ghost, full of wisdom and of good report (Acts 6:3-4). They were capable of preaching God's word and serving people. Serving the widows was their primary function. Many times, a person wants to become a Deacon because of power and control. It will become his church! We must be careful who we place in positions that the line of good stewardship is not crossed to personal ownership. Deacons have been allowed to gather so much power and control that the churches are being sold out to personal agenda. The life expectancy of a church is no more than 50 years with a wavering trend after the first ten years resembling a roller coaster. A lot of this is because we are not cautious about who gets placed as leaders within the new works.

Although the Bible only addresses Deacons and Ministerial positions in placement, I believe we must watch the other leaders we place as well. It is the duty of the church planter to guide and direct, but the planter must also maintain control without being controlling. We would be wise to not have leaders in a church before placing someone that is not spiritually ready into a position.

As we look into selecting our leaders, there will be people that show up and are eager to serve. Many of them may come to you with a history of serving other churches. Learn what you can about them from talking to them. Be sure you check to see that they are doctrinally in line with the work the Lord has sent you to do. God speaks of a group of people called the Nicolaitanes whose deeds He hates (Revelation 2:6). These are people that have gone from church to church, not able to get a strong enough following to start their own work but are strong enough to do some really bad damage to the mission God has you on. They are direct messengers of Satan coming to destroy what God is doing. They are people on assignment. They look and talk like Christians but they are surrounded by their own selfish ambitions to do things their way. They have God all figured out. Beware of anyone that thinks they have God figured out!

We have had people come into a new work and they seemed dedicated until you watch their tithing habits and their commitment to the work. If people are coming into the church and tithing to outside ministries as a main source of tithing, they are not supporting the work that is going on. These people are merely making a show. We had a man in a church that tithed two dollars in 7 months and then wanted to run the church. Make sure you look for the fruit of spiritual maturity as you move forward (Galatians 5:22-24). These people will not be doing things the way God has instructed us to do. Their rebellious actions to God's Word will reveal them...

1Timothy 3; and Titus 1 instruct us on the way we should elect leaders of the church. I would like to say first that these are two Pastoral Epistles that are designed to educating Pastors in selecting leaders. The Pastoral Epistles, though educational for all, deal directly with the selection of the church leaders. It is not healthy for churches to call Pastors based on worldly belief and with the carnality that exists in most churches. Many churches cannot properly discern what God's will is for them. God said that people would hold to the traditions of men as opposed to the commandments of God. The traditions and teachings of men will make the Word of God of no effect. This is taking place every day in the church. There are cries there are not enough Pastors willing to fill pulpits. There is just not enough money to pay our Pastor! May I be so bold as to say, most of these problems are self-inflicted. These churches have become a revolving door ministry for many pastors. The churches expect more from Pastors than they are willing to give. They want the pastor and His family to make big sacrifice and be the only ones to walk by faith. This evolves from the teachings that we choose who we want and decide who are the called messengers of God based on do they match up to what we think and what the denomination says. Though denominations serve a good purpose, God cares less about denomination than the human soul. The churches of today should carefully and objectively look at calling a Pastor and see what the Lord requires of them as well. This is an area that should be taught as the church is founded (1 Corinthians 9).

The denominational talk is that Paul was a tent maker. He was a bi-vocational minister. Paul didn't get money from the churches! Paul, although he was a tent maker, he was not a Pastor. He was an Apostle by his own admission. He was sent by God to start new works all over the place. If we look into 1 Corinthians chapter 9:7-14, we will see that Paul is writing to the church in Corinth and explaining what their duties are in providing for the Pastor. He did not take anything, lest they suffer but once the Pastor was there, it is was their duty to support him. We also find this in the book of Exodus as we see the tribe of Levi being formed and the duties of the tribe outlined. We can even read further into the Word and find that once the tithe from all the tribes was taken to the Tabernacle, 10 percent of the tithe was offered up to God and the Levites got the other 90 percent. Now if that won't rock the foundational ground of the commitment for what churches believe in Pastoral support, I don't know what can! Perhaps, the old argument, we just don't have enough rings a bell for some of us. The Book of Acts says that people sold their homes to give the money for the continuation of ministry. The intention of the scripture is to do what it takes to hear and carry the message of God no matter what you may have to give up. I would not suggest you beat up on people about selling their homes to do something for the church. God will have them do that, if need be. All I am saying is, when you leave the church plant, do your best to have people ready to provide for the Pastor and support them fulltime.

I am not ashamed to admit that we have some things we call distinctives within denominations. We were in church the other day and an Evangelist began to tell about how he was told by God to baptize his brother. This was significant as the man's brother was suffering with terminal cancer at the time. The man had accepted Christ and requested to be baptized. One of the old Doctrinal positions is Baptism by immersion. While I believe it is Biblical to baptize this way, I do believe God honors our obedience to the act of baptism. The Evangelist was told to use a bowl full of water and sprinkle the water on his brother's head. I asked him how that changed his theology about baptism. The Evangelist was not ordained or licensed either. (I'm sure that it doesn't make his brother any less baptized.) The response from the evangelist was simply "Exactly!"

These two scriptures outline the life and conduct of people in the desire to be in the office of Bishop and Deacon. I can assure you one thing; I had no desire to be a Pastor but God had a plan! There are many people who live a good life and can meet these qualifications. There are a lot of good people in the church. There are those that have much wealth that people like to get in position as an avenue to more money. There is so much that can be read into these scriptures about qualifications. It is the only area that describes the conduct of the Deacon's wife. In fact, the wording for the wife of the Deacon would take you straight back to the word "Diablo" which in Greek means Devil or Satan when it refers to the slanderous gossip that the wife must refrain from (1 Timothy 3:11).

There are issues of divorce that come from these scriptures. It would be better to see a divorced, born again believer serving in any of these offices as opposed to those meeting worldly qualifications and have never come to experience Jesus as their Savior. At least the born-again believer is forgiven by God. Who really cares what man has to say? God says the reason we are not to select, and He is talking to Pastors here, is that:

"For there are many unruly and vain talkers and deceivers, specially them of the circumcision:" Titus 1:10 (KJV)

He is referring to those caught up in religiosity or legalism in this verse.

God is not saying that these people shouldn't serve on account of their past experiences but because of the present performance of the religious legalists in the church. I am not sure that I can go along with the scriptures being interpreted as they are sometime interpreted. There are some that take this as a solid rule that women cannot serve in Pastoral roles and there are those that believe this issue is addressing the area of divorce. Through study, I am convinced that regardless of what we think, we must know that God calls Pastors and people to serve. We can either seek His wisdom in all matters or become pious and cold about them. A word of caution would be to check every situation and ask the Lord about it. Once the church begins to seek God, He will begin to do His work through them. If we are to take the critical text approach to interpreting the scriptures in these two letters, we can go back to the issues of polygamy being addressed. With the way we watched the fall of King Solomon and King David before him over the wife situation, it would be very practical for God to say one wife is fine because I created you to have one but no more. Women were never allowed to have more than one husband so there would never be a reason to address the marriage issue to them. Had God not intended for women to be used in Pastoral roles, He would have never sent Paul to help Lydia and we would still be hearing Paul's words of shout trying to figure out what God was doing to him (Acts 16:6-15).

God is no respecter of person and to give a person that has been divorced and remarried a different set of rules makes Him respect someone that hasn't had problems in a different light. God says there is neither male nor female in Christ (Galatians 3:26-29). I believe God can use who He wants, when and where He wants to accomplish what He wants. We simply must be willing, as church planters to pray over all these issues. They are sure to come up as you go along. We will eventually learn that we can be conservative and even fundamental in our beliefs but the liberality of the Love of God will begin to become evident in our lives. This doesn't make you a liberal or any leader you select a liberal either. This kind of love enables your leaders and others, as well as you to see people purely as the Lord sees them through Jesus.

It would be better for the sake of the Lord's work to have a person that is poor and hard working but loves God and meets the qualifications in Acts 6 to be a Deacon or church leader than it would for someone to meet the qualifications in 1 Timothy 3 or Titus 1 and does not have a relationship with God. A personal relationship with God, through Christ is essential in selecting your leaders. Hey, if you can find a rich person and they meet all the criteria listed in every place, get them! Don't sell God's church out by placing worldly leaders in charge.

CHAPTER EIGHT

We've got Work to Do! - Revelation 7:9-11

Revelation 7:9; *"After this I beheld, and, lo, a great multitude, which no man could number, of all nations, and kindreds and people, and tongues, stood before the throne, and before the Lamb, clothed with white robes, and palms in their hands:"*

As I read through the Word of God one day, I was drawn to Revelation 7:9. There it says that around the throne were gathered people of every tribe, nation and kingdom, to big in number to count. Reality hit me between the eyes as I realized I was looking at a picture of the raptured church. I was overwhelmed with the thought that, man, we've got some serious work to do!

Jesus gave us the Great Commission in Matthew 28. We know that the fall of man caused us to be born into a state of sin. Just how do we express that fall? In October 2002, Cheryl and I had the privilege of being at the Billy Graham School of Evangelism in the Metroplex in the Dallas area. It had been a great week with what people who are known today as some real spiritual giants. We had the opportunity to see and hear some men of God that we would have never gotten the chance to see or hear except on the radio. It gave us time to listen to what God has them doing in their ministries and how He has blessed them. We were going to see Dr Graham deliver God's message on the Thursday night meeting of the crusade. We went into the Texas stadium and it was not like any other stadium I had ever been in before. We walked out on the stairway and proceeded down the steps. Well, I was joking with some guys behind me about all good Baptists would have to sit up front that night. There was a big blue tarp covering the playing field, a long way below. As I turned to look for the next step, I missed it in the line of my bi-focals and began to fall forward. My wife was right in front of me, so naturally, I reached for her. Although I know she loves me dearly, she hurriedly moved so as not to be knocked over by my fall. I was going face first down these stairs not knowing where I was going to stop. When I finally stopped, it was in front of all the ministers that had been teaching us that day. As I got up, people ask me was I okay? My response was yes. My wife just took off across the front of the stadium seats and then decided to climb over a row to sit near some of the friends we had made there. (This school and crusade were real treats for us as we had managed somehow to bump the announcement that Billy Graham was coming to Texas to the bottom of the page of the December 31, 2001 Baptist Standard, as God gave us the first three quarters of the page in a newspaper with about 150,000 in circulation.) We never thought we would be on the same page with Billy Graham let alone be in a place to hear him speak. I had sprained my right wrist and my left ankle. This combination made it nearly impossible to do anything. The crusade was great and we really enjoyed the word of the Lord delivered through Dr Graham. What I learned about all this was, the fall of man was not a flat on the face kind of fall. This fall is one that is gradual that will only stop at the pits of hell unless we answer the tug in our heart from the Lord. The distance that people fall is different from someone else but the separation and the ultimate destiny could be the same. It was then that I realized that even those around us sidestep us during the fall we encounter and will walk off and leave us once we stop. As I said, my wife loves me dearly. I am convinced that she wouldn't want to see any harm done to me unless it was going to hurt her too! Is this the way it works? I was thinking that we so often are willing to stand until it might affect us, then we step out of the way. There is much uncertainty involved in the fall. Yes, my wife was there when my fall stopped. She asked the same question all people ask when someone has a mishap. Are you all right? No! I wasn't all right but my pride wouldn't let me say that I was messed up. I surely didn't want to let anyone know that I was physically hurting; after all, I was already embarrassed pretty bad. Maybe I suffered through some things I didn't need to suffer through as a result of my pride in refusing to admit I was hurt. I didn't want sympathy but I didn't anticipate climbing over chair rows either. I believe we are quick in asking if someone is hurt and when they respond with a no, we abandon them to fend for themselves. They are wounded and very vulnerable to falling again. Once a person gets up from this fall, it is up to us to help them to become spiritually well once again. This fall was not about my wife or my clowning, it was about God showing me that man is falling in a sloping downward trend with the bottom stop being Hell itself. We can, through our own testimony serve as a step to stop the downhill slide of someone that is sliding into Hell. The key is, in order to have a Testimony; you must first endure the test!

As we are going to be gathered around the Throne of Jesus, we will be worshipping Him throughout all eternity. We will all be together worshipping the only true and Living God, our Savior and Lord, Jesus Christ. Do you think that we will be hurting then? I think not! There is not going to be any kind of separation from God because of socio-economic or cultural barriers, which man has imposed. It will be all about serving Jesus. I am reminded when Jesus spoke to the scribes that there was virtue in the room to heal them all but only the paralytic lowered through the roof was healed because of faith.

We have a good friend that is a songwriter. He had written a song some years back but was able to have it recorded recently on a new CD from the Oak Ridge Boys. Rock Killough, from Greenville, Alabama wrote and sang about the problems of this world and playing the blame game with who is at fault. The bottom line to the song is, we are in trouble because of the "Absence of Love." Thanks to God and to Rock Killough for this song. Thanks to the Oaks for singing it and putting it out for the world to hear. What better time could we be hearing such a song? Our united praises to God should be started right here on earth. Oh, for the desire to see man love one another. Jesus said that we should love one another as He has loved us. Rock has also written another song that unlocks the door to every emotion we could ever have. Rock writes: "You've got to get the Love of Jesus in your heart." It is essential that we find and get this love and share it, without reservation, and become witnesses for Christ.

CHAPTER NINE

Be Encouraged - Philippians 4:11

Philippians 4:11-13; *"Not that I speak in respect of want: for I have learned, in whatsoever state I am, therewith to be content. I know both how to be abased and I know how to abound: everywhere and in all things I am instructed both to be full and to be hungry, both to abound and to suffer need. I can do all things through Christ which strengtheneth me."*

Cheryl and I are by no means experts about church planting. We cannot tell you the systematic ways of doing things. All we can do is share our experiences with you as you read through this book. We hope that you have found some nugget that you can hold on to as you serve the Lord.

One day, the Lord is subject to tell you it is time to go to church planting or if you're currently planting churches, back into Pastoral ministry again. You will be looking back at the past as we have in this book with great memories. God will have used you mightily. Whether you were successful in the plant or the elements tore you apart, it really makes no difference to the Lord. We know that God knew the outcome even before He sent you. He may have just wanted to stir His people a little bit or perhaps give them just one more chance. We will probably never know the answers to all these things in this lifetime and they won't matter on the other side.

We pray that this book can be an inspiration as we share with you how God led us to do things in planting new works. When it is time to return to Pastoral ministry, you will return with a deeper relationship and much stronger faith than when you initially left the Pastorate. I found through church planting I really knew nothing about being a Pastor to God's people because in so many ways I had not learned to follow first.

When things seem to be their darkest in times of church starting, you are on the brink of seeing a great break through in the Lord's work.

I am writing, as almost an after thought, upon completion of this book but feel that I must go on to share with you some things about finances of the church. God's way to finance the work He wants done is through His people. This is a hard trend to get people into and away from the ideology that they will be kind and generous and give God a tip on Sunday morning because He has been a good God this week. He talks to us in 1 Timothy 6:10,

"For the love of money is the root of all evil; which while some coveted after, they have erred from the faith, and pierced themselves through with many sorrows."

God wants His people to give and give willingly (2 Corinthians 8:12). The problem we have is the line of the love of money. Where does this line start in our lives? When you are driven by the need for money, money has just displaced God in your life? I want to share with you a testimony about us as we were in central Texas. There were many days we didn't have food in our house! There were times that people would bring food and leave it in the front hall of the house and never say they had done so. Many days the Lord would send someone by the house to bring us money ranging in amounts of 300 dollars to 2500 dollars and always on time! God saw to it that we did not need money to live. He provided everything. One little church we started had the power restored and the power company charged us a great rate for doing so. The power meter never turned a single revolution in 24 months. God says that He owns the world and the fullness thereof. You can hang your hat on that! God doesn't need the money the people have! God wants them to give. If they don't give, He will take it from them. All people will give to someone or God, it is their choice. This scripture that is so often justified in the minds of men is a big downfall when it comes to our work as church planters. People adopt a dangerous mindset thinking their money is so important that God is not going to provide when money givers leave the church. They allow the money issue to dominate a situation. God will send in money from places you would never believe it would come from. It is oftentimes like the Lord himself reaches out of your mailbox and hands you a check as He kisses you and blesses you. We were in a situation that an old church needed water but regulations for water and sewer systems had changed over the years, thus creating some potential problems. The lot was just too small for all the needs. As we were getting the old building back in shape, we attempted to buy the lot next door to the old church. The owner asked what we needed with it. We explained the water situation, as septic was already there. He laughed and told us to go and tie into his well just behind the building and get all the water we needed for the church. God doesn't need money; He needs warriors and that is what you are! In another situation of church starting, we became more innovative in capitalizing on resources but will save those thoughts for another book.

Keep your eyes on Jesus and believe. God will guide your footsteps. God says that He directs the footsteps of the righteous. Don't give up the walk of faith and lean to those things the world would have us to lean towards. It is a tough calling the Lord has brought you to consider but, He will give you the grace to get the job done.

Blessings!

Randy & Cheryl

Meet the Authors

Cheryl and Randy Heddings

Cheryl (Bigelow) and Randy Heddings grew up in the same small town along the Mississippi Gulf Coast. Cheryl was raised Catholic and Randy Lutheran. Home. Cheryl learned to hear the voice of God early in life, Randy later.

Cheryl and Randy met, married, and raised four children. When their third child graduated from high school, Cheryl and Randy realized they were called to Christian ministry.

Cheryl, Randy, and Jessica (twelve-year old daughter) went to central Texas to start new works. They went with no money, no demographic facts, and no church planting training. For the next two years they served God and followed His will only. In response, the Holy Spirit amazed them with His guidance of their ministry.

Made in the USA
Columbia, SC
24 January 2024